A Ladybird Bible Book

Daniel and Esther

Text by Jenny Robertson
Illustrations by Alan Parry

Scripture Union/Ladybird

Nebuchadnezzar, the king of Babylon, was so powerful he conquered many kingdoms, including the kingdom of Judah where the Jewish people lived. He captured the king and other important Jewish families and took them back to Babylon. Then he called his chief official. 'I want you to choose some of the new prisoners to serve me here at court. Teach them our language and let them eat food from the royal tables.'

So the chief official chose several young men including a handsome young prince called Daniel and his three friends, Shadrach, Meshach and Abednego.

At first Daniel and his friends were pleased, but there was one problem. 'We can't eat Babylonian food,' Daniel told the official. 'The God we serve has given us rules about the kind of things we eat. We would break them if we ate your meals.'

But the chief official didn't dare to disobey the king by allowing the young men to eat differently. So Daniel asked one of their guards for help.

'Please give us a trial period when we just get vegetables and water. Then see if we look fit or not at the end of ten days.'

The guard agreed. Ten days later the four young men looked fitter and healthier than everyone else who had been eating the king's food.

'All right, you can stay on your diet!' the guard told them. God had helped Daniel and his friends obey him.

Soon Daniel and his friends became well known at the king's court. They were clever and could help the king in all the decisions he had to make. Then one night Nebuchadnezzar had a dream which worried him so much he asked his magicians to tell him what it meant, but he wouldn't tell them what the dream was.

Of course no one could tell him what the dream meant if they didn't know what it was, but the king was furious with them.

'I'll have you all put to death. You're no good!' he exclaimed.

As soon as he heard about the king's verdict, Daniel rushed off to find his friends.

'Let's pray that God will show us the meaning of the king's dream,' he suggested.

That very night God showed Daniel what the dream was and what it meant. Daniel hurried to the king.

'God has showed me what your dream was,' he told Nebuchadnezzar. 'You saw a giant statue gleaming with gold and silver. As you watched, a stone fell on the statue and broke it into pieces. Then the stone grew into a mountain that covered the whole earth. The dream is

to show you that although human kings may be as powerful as that statue, God is even more powerful. One day he will send his own king to set up a kingdom which will never end.'

Nebuchadnezzar was very impressed. 'Your God is more powerful than any other,' he said. 'I'm going to put you in charge of all my advisers.'

Some time later Nebuchadnezzar had an enormous gold statue made which everyone had to worship.

'If anyone refuses to worship this statue he'll be thrown into a blazing furnace,' warned the king's officials, and all over Babylon everyone came and fell flat in front of the statue — everyone except Daniel's three friends, Shadrach, Meshach and Abednego.

'What's this?' demanded the king. 'I'll throw you into that furnace if you don't worship my statue. No one will be able to rescue you, not even your God.'

'We serve the true God, your Majesty,' answered Shadrach, Meshach and Abednego. 'We will worship only him, and whether he saves us or not we are not going to worship your statue.'

'Make the furnace seven times hotter,' yelled Nebuchadnezzar. 'Tie up these men and throw them into the furnace.'

The blaze was so hot it burnt the soldiers who pushed Shadrach, Meshach and Abednego into the furnace. The three friends toppled forward into the flames.

Suddenly Nebuchadnezzar jumped to his feet. 'Look, there are four people walking about completely unharmed right in the middle of the flames! And the fourth one is so splendid he must be an angel.' He went up to the furnace door and called, 'Shadrach, Meshach and Abednego, come out!'

The three friends walked calmly out of the blazing furnace completely unhurt.

'God sent his angel to save you!' declared Nebuchadnezzar. 'You risked your lives rather than disobey him. From now on no one is ever to speak disrespectfully of you or your God.'

Many years passed. Nebuchadnezzar died and a new king called Darius came to the throne. He soon decided that Daniel was so honest and trustworthy that he wanted to put him in charge of all his officials, too. That made the other officials jealous of Daniel. They thought of a plan to have him killed.

'Please sign this law,' they said to Darius. The law decreed that no one was to pray to any god except to King Darius himself for one whole month. Whoever did was to be thrown into a pit where lions were kept. Darius signed the law and the governors went away to spy on Daniel.

'The king can't alter the law now he's signed it,' they muttered. 'He'll have to throw Daniel to the lions because he will never pray to anyone except his Jewish god.'

They were right. Even though Daniel knew all about the new law he knelt down by his window which faced towards his homeland far away and prayed there quite openly three times a day, just as he always did.

The governors lost no time. They reported Daniel to the king, who had to obey the law he had signed, though he was sad about what would happen to Daniel. Daniel was flung into the pit where the lions snarled. The king sealed the entrance. There was no escape.

'Only your God can save you now,' the king cried, but he was so upset he lay awake all night thinking of Daniel. As soon as it was light he hurried to the pit.

'Daniel, was your God really able to save you from the lions?' he called.

To his joy he heard Daniel's voice. 'Long live your Majesty! God sent his angel and stopped the lions hurting me.'

So the king had Daniel pulled out of the pit at once. 'Now everyone in my vast empire must respect your God who does such wonderful things!' he declared.

Daniel never went back home to Judah but he stayed faithful to God till the end of his life.

The years went by. Daniel and his friends died, but their children and grandchildren still lived in Babylon. A new king called Xerxes ruled over them now.

One day the king decided he wanted a new queen. He ordered all the most beautiful girls in the kingdom to come to his palace in Susa so that he could choose the one he liked the best to be his wife.

When the girls arrived they were taken to the women's quarters and given a special beauty treatment for a whole year before the king saw them. One of the girls was a young Jewish woman called Esther. She was an orphan and she lived with her cousin Mordecai who had brought her up.

'Don't tell anyone that we're related or that you're Jewish,' he warned Esther when she went to the palace.

At last it was time for Esther to be taken to the king. She looked so beautiful that Xerxes fell in love with her at once. 'You are the wife I have been looking for!' he exclaimed. 'You shall be my queen!'

He put the royal crown on Esther's head and that night he held a great feast in her honour. Everyone in the kingdom had a holiday to celebrate the wedding.

Meanwhile Mordecai had taken a job in the palace. While he was working there he overheard two of the king's guards plotting to murder the king.

'Xerxes must be warned about this,' thought Mordecai. 'I must tell Esther.'

Esther told the king what Mordecai had discovered. 'Two of your guards are planning to kill you, your Majesty,' she warned him.

The king held a complete investigation and the two men were arrested and hanged.

'Make sure that all this is noted down in the palace records,' ordered the king. 'Mordecai has saved my life.'

Soon afterwards King Xerxes issued another order. 'All my officials must bow down to Haman the new Prime Minister.' So everyone began bowing to the ground whenever Haman appeared. Only Mordecai refused.

'I'm a Jew,' he explained to the other officials. 'I only bow in worship to God.'

Haman was so furious he went to the king.

'Your Majesty, in your empire there are people called Jews who refuse to obey your orders,' he said. 'They should all be executed.'

Xerxes agreed and sent messengers throughout the empire to say that on the thirteenth day of that very month every single Jewish man, woman and child was to be killed.

When Mordecai heard the news he tore his clothes to shreds. He put on pieces of rough cloth and covered his head with ash as a sign of grief. Then he walked through the city to the palace with tears streaming down his face.

Queen Esther sent a trusted servant out to speak to Mordecai and find out what had made him so upset.

Mordecai told the servant what the king had done. 'Ask Esther to beg the king for mercy,' he added.

But that was not easy for Esther, for the Babylonian law said that no one could go into the king's rooms without permission, and the king had been too busy even to speak to Esther for a whole month. She was in danger of being put to death if she went to speak to the king without being asked, unless he was merciful and held out his golden sceptre to her. She sent an urgent message back to Mordecai. 'Gather all the Jews in Susa together and spend the next three days praying for me. Don't eat or drink anything. Just pray, and my maids and I will do the same. Then I'll go to the king and if he puts me to death, well, I shall just have to die.'

So Mordecai and his friends went without food and prayed for Esther — and Esther prayed too. Then on the third day she put on her royal robes and went to the king. She waited in the hall facing the throne and the king looked up. To Esther's relief he held out the golden sceptre.

'What can I do for you?' he asked as Esther touched the sceptre.

'Will you and Haman come and have dinner with me tonight?' Esther asked.

So the king and Haman dined with Esther and then the king asked Esther again what he could do for her.

'Come and dine with me tomorrow and I shall tell you then,' Esther replied.

Haman was delighted that Queen Esther had given him a second invitation, but as he left the palace he saw Mordecai, and, as usual, Mordecai wouldn't bow down to him.

'How I hate that man!' Haman exclaimed. 'I won't enjoy my power until he's dead!'

'Then ask the king to have him executed at once,' suggested his friends, and Haman agreed.

That night Xerxes couldn't sleep, so to pass the time till daylight he ordered his servant to read the official records aloud to him. When the reader reached the report about the plot that Mordecai had discovered, Xerxes remembered that he had never rewarded Mordecai for saving his life. At that moment Haman burst in to ask to have Mordecai put to death. Before he could speak the king said, 'Ah, Haman, you're just in time to give me some advice. There's someone I want to reward. What do you suggest?'

'The king must mean me!' thought Haman, so he said, 'Order one of your most important noblemen to dress the man in royal robes and lead him on horseback through the city announcing that this is how your Majesty treats someone you want to honour.'

'A good idea, Haman,' approved Xerxes. 'Hurry and dress Mordecai in my royal robes and lead him through the city.'

So the furious Haman had to honour Mordecai instead of having him put to death.

That evening the king and Haman had dinner with Esther again and the king asked Esther once more what he could do to make her happy.

'Please save me and my people because we're all about to be killed,' Esther said.

'Who would dare kill you, Queen Esther?' demanded Xerxes.

'Haman is the enemy of my people,' Esther replied.

'Not only that, but he's actually built a high gallows on which to hang Mordecai the Jew who saved your Majesty's life,' one of the king's officials added.

'Hang Haman on his own gallows,' ordered the king. So Haman was led out and executed, and then Esther told the king that Mordecai was really her adopted father.

'He can come to my palace and be second in the empire to me,' declared the king.

So Mordecai came to the palace, and together Esther and Mordecai begged Xerxes to save the Jews who were still in danger because of the law Haman had persuaded the king to pass.

'I can't change my proclamation, but I can allow your people to fight and defend themselves,' said the king.

So throughout the empire the Jews were allowed to fight the soldiers who came to execute them. Instead of being killed themselves they all managed to put their enemies to death.

The next day they celebrated with parties and feasts the victory which had saved their lives. They gave presents to one another and made sure that the poor people who couldn't afford presents, or even enough food, received special gifts. Mordecai sent letters throughout the kingdom telling everyone to make this celebration every year. To this very day, Jewish people give one another presents on a special holiday called Purim which they celebrate to remember how Queen Esther and her cousin Mordecai saved their people from the destruction planned by Haman long ago.

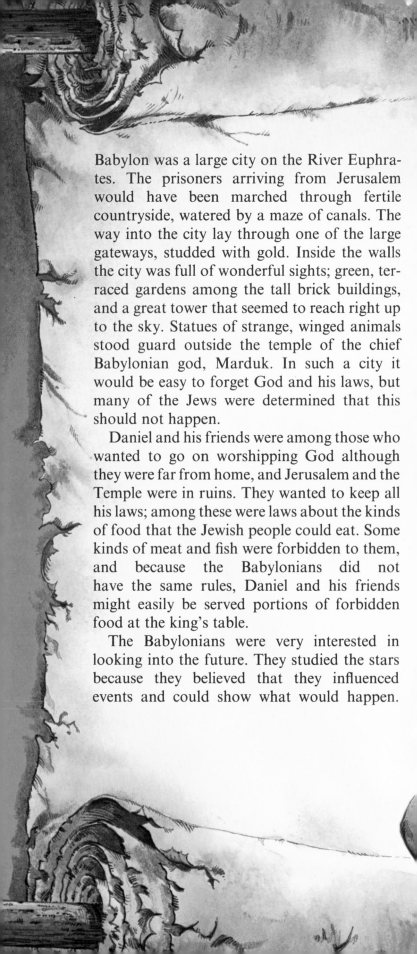

Babylon was a large city on the River Euphrates. The prisoners arriving from Jerusalem would have been marched through fertile countryside, watered by a maze of canals. The way into the city lay through one of the large gateways, studded with gold. Inside the walls the city was full of wonderful sights; green, terraced gardens among the tall brick buildings, and a great tower that seemed to reach right up to the sky. Statues of strange, winged animals stood guard outside the temple of the chief Babylonian god, Marduk. In such a city it would be easy to forget God and his laws, but many of the Jews were determined that this should not happen.

Daniel and his friends were among those who wanted to go on worshipping God although they were far from home, and Jerusalem and the Temple were in ruins. They wanted to keep all his laws; among these were laws about the kinds of food that the Jewish people could eat. Some kinds of meat and fish were forbidden to them, and because the Babylonians did not have the same rules, Daniel and his friends might easily be served portions of forbidden food at the king's table.

The Babylonians were very interested in looking into the future. They studied the stars because they believed that they influenced events and could show what would happen.